How to run a Stately Home

How to run a Stately Home

John, Duke of Bedford

In collaboration with GEORGE MIKES

Illustrated by FFOLKES

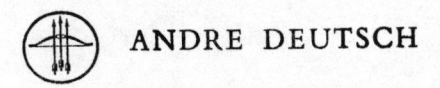

ANDRE DEUTSCH

First published 1971 by
André Deutsch Limited
105 Great Russell Street London WC1

Copyright © 1971 by John, Duke of Bedford
and George Mikes
All Rights Reserved

Printed in Great Britain by
Ebenezer Baylis and Son Ltd
The Trinity Press, Worcester, and London

ISBN 0 233 95848 7

TO MY WIFE
with love and gratitude.
She does all the work.

Contents

First steps for beginners *11*
How not to . . . *17*
On stateliness and homeliness *25*
On being a Duke *31*
On being commercial *41*
Why do they come? *49*
Dinner with a Duke *57*
The circuit *65*
The Commonwealth *71*
The Europeans *75*
Entrance fee *79*
Against Stately Homes *85*
On food *91*
Household problems *99*
On ghosts *105*
On lions and monkeys *113*
Fishing *121*
Postscript *125*

First steps for beginners

'How do you set about opening a Stately Home? What are the qualifications you need?'

I have been asked these questions hundreds, if not thousands, of times. People regard me as the founding father of the Stately Home business which, I am sorry to say, I am not. Many Stately Homes were open to the public in the eighteenth century and Woburn Abbey itself was already open in the nineteenth, every Monday, 'for gentlemen and foreigners' (I am not sure whether this was meant as a special courtesy to foreigners or as a clear indication that they are not gentlemen). But I am perhaps one of the Big Five, and it is possible that I make more noise than many of my confrères and competitors. Be that as it may, I get so many inquiries regarding the possibilities, problems and intricacies of Stately Homes that I feel a considerable proportion – perhaps even, or so it seems at times, the majority – of the population contemplate turning their homes stately. I am thus persuaded that a handbook on the subject is overdue, and I propose to write it.

Qualifications first: there are two which are essential. The first, which will be confirmed by any shrewd accountant or business man, is that you must be at least a little mad. The second is that you must love your house and its contents beyond anything else in this world.

If you don't have this deep-rooted passion for your house, don't try. If you can no longer afford to live in it privately, find some capital and hand it over to the National Trust who will run it efficiently, with deep-frozen good taste, and it will stop being a house and become a monument or a museum. But if you combine a good touch of mania with the natural animal instinct to protect your and your ancestors' Tom Tiddler's ground, go ahead.

You will then find that being permanently in the red is less alarming than you supposed (the bank rather likes it provided you pay up finally or occasionally), and that preserving what is fine and beautiful, and enabling other people to see it and enjoy it is most rewarding. Now that I come to think of it, I should have added a third qualification: you must like your fellow men. You are about to undertake a challenging business, and you can be sure of constant worry, so if you don't take real pleasure in seeing other people enjoy themselves you may become a bit frayed. If you do, then realizing that you are there to serve your customer, and to serve him well, will be stimulating; and if that attitude comes naturally to you, you are on the road to success.

Now for the question 'How do you set about opening a Stately Home?' I shall treat my readers – or pupils, if you

First steps for beginners

like – as absolute beginners, prompted to do so by the naïveté of their questions. I am so often asked: how many Rembrandts do you need before going Stately? Is a gold-plated dinner service necessary?

You do not need any Rembrandts at all, and a gold-plated dinner service even less.

What, then, *is* the very first thing you need?

I can answer this question firmly, without a moment's hesitation: the first thing you need is good loos, and plenty of them.

To many people, no doubt, this will sound cynical. I have been described as cynical before. But I started out as an idealist. I too, when wondering what I should offer the public, had paintings and objects of *vertu* in mind. I too was foolish enough to think that loos were of secondary importance. Having learnt my lesson, however, I passed it on freely and generously to newcomers to the business. They disbelieved me, shook their heads, smiled, pitied me for my lack of fine feelings. All of them came back very soon, clothed in sackcloth and ashes, to apologize and admit that I had been right.

Of course I am right. Why do people visit Stately Homes? The reasons vary (more of this later) but a considerable majority do so because they own cars. They have cars and they want to drive them, and they would feel silly if they were not driving them *somewhere*. A Stately Home provides a destination: it is excellent for this purpose. Now, to see a Rembrandt or a Canaletto, beautiful furniture, fine china, or even a gold-plated dinner service, may give pleasure; but it is not a biological necessity after a long drive. To visit the loo is.

I have just looked through the letters I have received from my visitors over the years. More than three hundred of a large bunch refer to loos. I have not bought a Rembrandt since I opened my house to the public but I have had to build loo-block after loo-block. And I am going on building them. If things continue at the present rate, my loo-blocks will equal my house in cubic feet by 1984; by 2001 the ratio will be 2:1 in favour of the loos. (But by then it will be cubic metres.)

Even old hands like myself keep making mistakes. I had learnt by experience that the first thing people do on arriving at a Stately Home is visit the loo, so before I opened my Game Reserve I built what I thought was a generous allotment of loos near the entrance. I doubted if they were sufficient in number but I hoped for the best. To my surprise I found that there were far too many. There they stand, unvisited and unloved. Because – such are the mysteries of human nature – those who visit Game Reserves, unlike all the others, want to go to the loo at the end and not at the beginning. So I had hastily to erect a monumental loo-block at the end of the round.

What do people actually do in these loos? beginners may ask. I am not sure about the men but I can vouch for the women: they wreck the place, throw paper about, damage the installations and pinch the chains. Why? I am not sure. Perhaps there is a hidden streak of violence in the female psyche which breaks loose in the loos (no pun

First steps for beginners

intended) of Stately Homes more readily than anywhere else. Perhaps this phenomenon is an organized demo of the Women's Lib movement against the aristocracy. But perhaps, on second thoughts, it has no political significance and is connected with the fact that it is usually the women, not the men, who take the children in with them. All I can be sure of is that newcomers to the industry should use the heaviest concrete for the *Ladies* and that the chains should be ships' anchor-chains bought from vast old Cunard liners now being turned into American universities.

Very well, you may say impatiently, your advice has sunk in. Loos are important. All right, they are *most* important. But do you mean to say that nothing else really matters?

No, I do not. While loos must come first, they would not take you far without teas and car-parks.

A Stately Home with excellent loos, good teas served at a reasonable price, and sufficient car-parks (near the loos and the tea-rooms) will prosper. If you provide these three commodities, then – according to my computer – 87·3 per cent of your visitors will not notice if you have no house at all.

This is not to say that a Stately House will not come in handy; but stately loos, good teas and plenty of parking space – these are indispensable.

How not to...

A negative definition may not be every philosopher's dream but I often find it most illuminating. So, before going any further with my positive instructions, I shall inform my pupils how *not* to run a Stately Home.

Perhaps the most important of all rules is this: never pray for good weather. You may be a particular favourite of the gods, your prayer may be answered and you may get a truly lovely day. In that case all your would-be (or rather might-have-been) customers go and enjoy that lovely day by the sea.

Next in importance: do not be beastly to your customers. Some people – quite a sizeable minority – like being treated like dirt. They like to feel that they are unimportant and merely on sufferance wherever they may be. They love to look small in the shadow of true greatness. These people will enjoy the treatment allotted to them in certain Stately Homes, but they are a minority. The majority want to get value – or at least some value – for their money.

Do not employ guides who do not know their job; or who mutter and mumble so that no one knows what they are talking about. But even ignorant and inarticulate

They love to look small in the shadow of true greatness

How not to . . .

guides are just permissible provided they are kind and courteous. The worst type of guide is the man or woman who appears superior – part and parcel of a grand and superior establishment where every ordinary mortal ought to feel overawed – and talks down to people. He rushes through his lines, does not encourage questions and when they come he answers them snubbingly. He gives orders, such as 'Move along!' or 'Shut that door, will you?' in a cool and extremely refined voice. He will inevitably make the visitor feel that he is on a conveyor belt; that the owners only want his money and the sooner he clears out the better.

Keep your Stately Home open every day and all day. I know a few places which are open, say, on Wednesday mornings and Thursday afternoons between Easter and Whitsun and then on Monday afternoons and Friday mornings between August Bank Holiday and St Crispin's Day. Nine people out of ten will arrive on the wrong day or at the wrong time on the right day, will swear and fume and go away, never to return.

But it is really the *attitude* that matters. For a large number of people opening their houses to the vulgar plebs, the *hoi polloi*, is the last resort. A few lucky people can afford to keep up their palaces without public help. That is perfectly all right. But if you do open your Stately Home to the common clay, to the so-called ordinary people, do not do it in an atmosphere of despair. Do not say – even to your wife, even to yourself – that although the money and the tax advantages are welcome,

How to run a Stately Home

how you wish you didn't have to let the actual people in. Those people are extremely unlikely just to send in their money by postal order to support you. They *will* come. So you might as well make the best of it – even enjoy it. That is surely only common sense, yet there are some owners who feel that once they have humiliated themselves by opening their house to the vulgar masses they have done enough. They firmly believe that with their *suffering* they are paying a high price and they deserve salvation. As long as this opening is *unpleasant* to them they are doing their painful duty: whether all those common people are enjoying themselves or not, is *their* business.

Say you have six Rembrandts, eight Titians, a dozen Tintorettos and three Raphaels before you give in to pressure, sigh deeply, and agree to open your house to the public. Do not go and sell all – or almost all – of your pictures before the opening; do not hide your really good stuff, furniture, china, carpets, etc and put only the rubbish on show. As I have said, many people will not notice even if you do not have a house at all; a lot will not be able to tell good stuff from bad and – as long as it is presented in a sufficiently pompous manner – will admire anything. But a number of people *do* notice and *do* care, and quite a few will know more about such things than you do. A poor and denuded Stately Home will be visited – but only once. People will never return and that's deadly. They may not be expert in the arts; but they will feel that they are unwelcome and there on sufferance, and who wants to repeat or talk up that experience?

How not to . . .

Once you decide to open your Stately Home to the public, you might as well stop regarding your customers as your triumphant enemies. They are clients, not an invading army – as you may be inclined to feel. I know many owners of Stately Homes who think – no, they do not *think*, they are convinced – that it is their right to live in a castle. After all they have gone to the right public schools, then to Oxford or Cambridge, served in the right regiments and were born in the right families, so it is an outrageous injustice that they have to let all these people in to trample on their lawn and interfere with the smooth running of their lives. Their only compensation is to treat their customers like dirt. Or if they are not angry, they are patronizing: let these good people see how the great families live. What a privilege for them!

But the good people – very often – see it very differently. They see the old furniture, the uncomfortable sofas and horrible, stiff armchairs; they walk through the unheated and unheatable rooms; they realize how far the dining-room is from the ridiculously old-fashioned kitchen. In other words they see how badly the rich live and that makes them happy. Thank goodness they do not have to live in a Stately Home!

If you are one of these old-fashioned, last-resort type of Stately Home owners, I would like to remind you of one of the great sages and philosophers of our century, Mrs Sophie Tucker. She said: 'I been rich; I been poor. Rich is better.' Few wiser words have ever been spoken. But remember: it is the people trampling your lawn, the vulgar plebs and the common masses who make it possible for you to remain rich.

What about myself? Do I practise what I preach? I think I do. First of all, like Sophie Tucker, I too have been poor and know that it is incomparably better to be better off. I do not doubt that I owe my good fortune to those people who come to see my garden, my Game Reserve, my house, my pictures. On top of it all, *they* say that they are grateful to me. How often do they tell me when I meet them in the grounds or in the rooms: 'Thank you very much... we are most grateful to you... But for you we could never have seen these pictures...'

I always reply: '*I* thank you. But for you I could not go on seeing these pictures myself.'

And then – I must confess to an unfashionable and uncynical emotion. I blush to say so, but I do like people. Indeed, people give me more pleasure than houses, china, silver and paintings – although I love and cherish all these things too. After all, I could hardly take against people when I like to think that we – my family and I – are people too.

What about privacy? Some Stately Homes are built in such a way that you cannot have any while the public is there, and that must be trying. Mine is different, and ideally yours should be different too so that even if, like me, you only rarely long for privacy, you can enjoy it when you want it.

Since I am not a withdrawing, misanthropic person –

How not to . . .

not the recluse type – I find it hard to understand those people who complain that after a certain time, if you become too well known, your face does not belong to you any more. I do not quite see the meaning of this phrase. I am not in love with my own face and if the public want to have it – or have a share in it – they can have it. My feelings are exactly the opposite of those described: I like being recognized and greeted by people; I enjoy being known and talked to. Only very rarely do I feel the need to hole up in my own quarters or to go abroad, where I can claim the ownership of my face again.

Far from feeling degraded at having to share my Stately Home with people, I feel flattered that they seem eager to share it with me. I have thirty-two sitting-rooms and I have never felt that I really *need* thirty-two sitting-rooms. Perhaps some of my fellow Stately Home owners know how to sit in thirty-two sitting-rooms (either concurrently or consecutively, as the saying goes) but I have no idea. Indeed, I am so busy, particularly during the season, that I have no time to sit down at all. Not in one single, solitary sitting-room. Let alone in thirty-two.

On stateliness and homeliness

I think it is a fair definition to say that a Stately Home is a place which is neither Stately nor a Home.

Certainly there are a few exceptions. Some houses opened to the public are stately; others are homely. Extremely few are both. Yes, on the whole, my definition stands.

Some very ordinary houses have been opened to the public and called Stately Homes but it is not this aspect of the matter which I have in mind. Even if a house was magnificent in every way when built, its condition must have deteriorated in the course of time. And, alas, this deterioration does not need the passing of centuries but happens at frightening speed. Repairs are ruinously expensive. So Stately Homes decay and threaten to disintegrate and the way of life for which they were built, which was the essence of their stateliness, becomes impossible to maintain. They may still be beautiful – even a ruin can be beautiful – but they become less and less stately.

It is hard for me to look around my domain with pride and pleasure – even if I were given to such sentiments – and whisper to myself with deep satisfaction: 'All this belongs to me!' My grandfather could do it and perhaps actually did it, but I know that this self-satisfied whisper would not be true. I must confess that it is difficult to look at any part of the buildings, however pleasing or even magnificent, with an objective eye, just drinking in its beauty. I always look with anxiety to see if anything needs repair.

Many of these huge, old-fashioned houses are dreary and uncomfortable inside. A home is primarily a place where you can sit down in a cosy corner in a comfortable armchair, put your feet up, feel warm, be alone and forget about the world. Stately Homes require too much work just to keep them going and the moments of rest and complete relaxation are few and far between. And even if you find the time, you can rarely find the cosy corner. You may have thirty-two sitting-rooms but you are extremely unlikely to have a corner in any of them which any electrician, motor mechanic or solicitor would call cosy. Sometimes you feel sad about this, but more often than not you don't worry about it. By the time the day is over you are so tired that you are ready to forget your thirty-two sitting-rooms and – even more to the point – your twenty-two dining-rooms, cosy or not. You just sit down somewhere – any old chair of the Louis Seize period or even the late Directoire style will do, under a fading Paolo Veronese or a Gentile da Fabriano – and have two soft-boiled eggs on a tray.

If this business is so arduous – you may ask – why am I persuading you to open up your Stately Home? Well, let

Doing nothing under my Rembrandts and Canalettos

me make myself clear: I am not persuading you, I am simply telling you that *if* you want to do it, this is the right way of going about it. But even so, the business has its compensations. First of all, as I have said, I enjoy meeting people. Then, in spite of all the hard work, I have a more interesting life than I would have in an old-fashioned world when I would idle about surrounded by a host of servants, taking my Rembrandts and Canalettos for granted – indeed, hardly noticing them. I now spend my life not only among people, but also fully aware of pictures and furniture, in a climate of art, tradition and history. I meet the great experts of various fields and I find my life rewarding.

But I should not be absolutely frank if I did not confess that I sometimes wonder why I am doing this. Would it not be much better to lead a relaxed life in a comfortable flat, without having to employ people and to run a business? It is very gratifying to own three thousand ancient tomes of great rarity, but I never read a single one. The books I do read are much more recent publications, frequently paperbacks, costing merely fifty new pence. When I contemplate the volumes in my library I never think of the profound spiritual pleasure they have given me because they have not given me any spiritual pleasure, profound or otherwise. I think of the melancholy fact that it cost me £3,000 to have the books cleaned and repaired.

So why – I ask myself in those rare moments of doubt – yes, why do I go on? The only convincing answer I can give myself comes from a book I read recently (*not* from

On stateliness and homeliness

my own, grand library of huge tomes) about the territorial imperative. It all started with the monkeys – I learnt – who each insisted on having his own special, private place up in the trees of the primordial forests. We humans have inherited this healthy and natural instinct from our ancestors: we must each have our own place. This territorial imperative is, basically and ultimately, the impulse that makes me go on fighting. I want my own place, this place happens to be it, and I am determined to keep it. I am the owner (or half-owner) of a magnificent Stately Home; I am also the monkey on the tree.

On being a Duke

Ideally the house you open to the public should be a large – possibly even a vast – edifice. I know that I have said that the house is not really important because about eighty per cent of the people do not care about it and many of them would not even notice if you had no house at all but camped in a tent at the far end of your park. This is true. But the remaining twenty per cent is a large minority; besides, most of the majority at least *look* at your house from a distance and they like to look at something immense, preferably preposterous.

The question then inevitably arises: what sort of man ought you to be if you wish to open an immense and preposterous house? I have given thorough and conscientious consideration to this problem and I advise you: be a Duke. It is incomparably easier for the Duke of Someplace to make a success of his Stately Home than for Mr Jones or Mr Smith.

I have touched upon this subject in an earlier work.* People often ask me, I said, if I like being a Duke. And I

---

* *The Duke of Bedford's Book of Snobs*, by John, Duke of Bedford, in collaboration with George Mikes, Peter Owen. Essential reading for all educated people.

answered – still answer – yes, I do. Some – the more straightforward ones – also ask me: do I know that being a Duke is an anachronism? Yes, I know that too. There is no contradiction in that: one may enjoy an anachronism. The advantages of being a Duke may be completely undeserved but they are numerous and enormous. I enjoy these advantages and I shall never be found in the forefront of any revolutionary movement dedicated to abolishing the peerage.

My feelings and thoughts on this subject have not changed much since 1965. People, my visitors, still treat me as one of the more interesting exhibits. Since I wrote the above-mentioned lines, I have added a Game Reserve to my place. It has proved to be successful and the lions are among the most popular sights in my zoo. But I seem to be even more interesting than the lions. I can't compete with the monkeys, but I beat the lions hands down. At least, I do not think I am going too far or am being immodest when I claim to be the most interesting lion in my zoo.

I honestly do not know why people should care to see me. I am astonished. But the point is that they do. I walk around and talk to people. They seem to be as pleased to see me as I am to see them. I go behind the counter and sell souvenirs and books. Whenever I do the selling the turnover goes up by fifty per cent.

Part of the explanation is that not everybody is keenly interested in eighteenth-century French furniture or in seventeenth-century Chinese porcelain, but a person is a

The most interesting lion in my zoo

person. As I have remarked before, the place only partly belongs to me; but I belong wholly to the place. As so often happens, a man's possessions do not belong to him, he belongs to his possessions. I, at least, realize that this is the position and accept it with pleasure.

I should not go so far as to say that everybody likes me. There are three main groups who object to me.

1. The people who think the aristocracy should live in a cobweb and rot peacefully and quietly away. The era of the aristocracy is over, so we should moulder away in ancient castles, preferably in their towers, chewing over past glories until we fade away unnoticed. The fact that I work as hard as any of my visitors never enters these critics' heads. And if it does it is just a disturbing factor: I am not playing my part properly. A modern aristocrat should not work hard. That does not fit the picture at all. He should be in a state of gentle decay; he should be peacefully disintegrating among the mementoes of a great past, brooding and bearing grudges but otherwise doing nothing.

2. A small number of people make extensive and aggressive efforts to show me that they are not impressed; that my being a Duke means nothing to them. I know only too well that it is through no merit of mine that I was born a Duke – which, by the way, I was not. But it is not my fault either. I had no say in the matter one way or another. I know perfectly well that there are a large number of excellent people for whom my title has absolutely no meaning; but they are not the people who

On being a Duke

go to any lengths to prove that they are not impressed. The genuinely indifferent are always as courteous to me as they are to everybody else. It is inverted snobs who go out of their way to be nasty, and these are the worst snobs of all – although I acknowledge their flattery with gratitude.

3. The third group is, in a way, the opposite of group number one. They are members of the old-fashioned nobility and gentry and their friends, who are firmly convinced that rich aristocrats have a right to the grand life even if they become poor aristocrats as a result of enjoying it. They have no doubt whatsoever that the heroic deeds of the glorious past – which in many cases were the origin of their ennoblement – entitle them and their descendants to special privileged treatment by society.

These people regard me as their *bête noir*. I am not *their* favourite lion. How often have I heard the contemptuous and scornful remark from one of my fellow Stately-Home owners: 'People like coming to my place because I am not commercial like you.' I nod and say nothing. A year later they close down shop and castle. Not being commercial may be noble and distinguished; but it does not take you far in this commercial age. I shall have more to say about this subject of commercialism; here I only wish to remark that I plead guilty. Even guiltier than the charge-sheet says I am. I am not only commercial, I am also a manufacturer. A manufacturer of news. About myself. A place like mine needs publicity. As I need several hundred thousand people to come and visit my place every year, I must remind them somehow that I am still alive and that my home is still open. I do not relish the scorn of the peerage – or part of the peerage – but I have no doubt whatsoever that it is much better to be looked down on than to be overlooked. And anyway I have long been looked down on by most of the peerage for another reason, so I have little to lose. I do not hunt. I dislike the idea of killing anything for pleasure, and that isn't easily forgiven in the upper reaches of British society. To many people it probably came as no surprise, after that, to learn that I could sink to promoting my business; while as for me – my lack of sporting spirit had given me plenty of practice in living with disapproval.

In what ways have my ideas changed since I last spoke about this subject? I still like being a Duke; I still enjoy being Top of the Pops or, at least, being one of the top ten. I am still there because it is so difficult to find the other nine to make up the list. The notorious film star and the famous stage actress of past decades are dead. Who cares about them? The rich executive, the brilliant and successful businessman – he too has lost a great deal of his glamour. We have had too much talk about money. And while I should not say that sex is out, the sex-symbol, the alluring female – whatever the size of her bosom – is also becoming a bit of a bore. So the aristocracy still has a chance of holding its place in the charts.

But I, personally, have never really been impressed with myself and with my rank, and in the last few years I have grown to love the world less, not more. There are no

Becoming a bit of a bore

spiritual values today and the rat race is becoming more and more depressing. In that respect Stately Homes in their hey-day were responsible for establishing true artistic values. In the days when these castles and palaces were built and furnished, people at least knew something about art and appreciated beauty. Today the loveliest and most exciting art treasures are bought as *investments*. They are acquired because they may go up in price and they are cherished because they cost so much. Even a generation ago Velasquez was admired for his own sake as one of the greatest painters who has ever lived; today he is worshipped because his works fetch more than £200,000. In any case, where is the non-expert nowadays who can tell a good Velasquez from a bad Velasquez? Or, for that matter, a good Velasquez from a bad . . . well, fill in the name of any mediocre painter you can think of.

Most people think it is wonderful to have a title and live in a large house, and I agree that it is better than being poor. Poverty is awful. It is good to have known poverty and to have got rid of it. But material things do not give a great deal of satisfaction in themselves and possessions mean a tremendous amount of responsibility. Young people – or at least a reasonable number of them – know that the views of the older generation are bunkum. They genuinely do not care about possessions and titles and they are not impressed. I, too, know that a man's real value is in his head. I should prefer a stately head to a stately home. But only a few of us have been given the choice.

But in spite of the young, the general climate of opinion

On being a Duke

has changed less in snobbery than in almost anything else. I repeat: this suits me. I was born a Lord; then I became a Marquess; finally I became a Duke. I used somewhat naïvely to think that in spite of all these changes in my status I had remained one and the same person. Not at all. How silly it was to believe that. To judge by the reactions of a great many people, when I became a Duke, I was not only reborn; I was born at last.

On being commercial

I have never heard of an artist being attacked for being artistic or a writer for being literary; a priest for being religious; a general for being military. But I, who run a business, am constantly attacked for being commercial. Before opening your own Stately Home you had better remember something which most people seem to forget: that the Stately Home business *is* a business. And there is not much point in attacking a business for being commercial.

The Stately Home business is not Big Business in the sense that ICI or General Motors are; nevertheless, it is big enough and not a game for bungling amateurs. When I inherited Woburn quite a few people tried to persuade me that it was not worth even sorting out the junk (as they put it). Death duties would kill me, I was told, and there was absolutely nothing to be done except to take my hat and walk out. Some optimists valued the 'junk' at £300,000 – not a serious sum when put against the five million pounds of death duties looming on the horizon. Undeterred, I sorted the junk out. It soon appeared, even to the pessimists, that the total value of the junk could not possibly be under one million pounds. Today, fifteen years

How run to a Stately Home

later, the junk is valued at eight million pounds. So it was worthwhile sorting it out.

How big a business is Woburn today? The place costs more than £300,000 a year to run, not much less than £1,000 a day. I rent my place from the Trustees for £30,000 a year and my insurance bill is £35,000 a year. So I have £65,000 expenses before I open my gates and before I have paid out one single penny in wages. At the height of the season I employ about three hundred people – so wage bills come into the picture, too. Without going into too many details, I should like to mention that I also have more than fifty antique dealers on the premises and I have to feed my lions and giraffes (they have healthy appetites). You cannot earn this sort of money just by keeping quiet, being unobtrusive and modest, and cultivating all the noble and aristocratic virtues, the most outstanding of which is to be unconcerned with that filthy stuff called money. Many Americans fly over to Britain and high on their list is a visit to Woburn. They would not put it there if my wife and I were not lucky enough to be interviewed quite frequently on American television and thus be given free advertisements which, in the normal way, would cost several million dollars. And people in this country would forget about me if I did not remind them of my existence by making a constant noise.

So I am accused of conducting my business on commercial lines. I might be forgiven if I did my work in an inefficient, amateurish way. To be engaged in business is

On being commercial

bad enough but to do it badly is, at least, compatible with ducal dignity. To do it well is unforgivable.

And it is not only the aristocracy (with the new-rich bankers, plastics manufacturers, etc thrown in) who condemn me for being commercial but quite a sizeable minority of ordinary people as well. They, too, feel that a Duke should live in an ivory tower, be cool and contemptuous of the masses and keep his castle to himself. They do not realize that the only way of keeping a castle nowadays, for most of us, is to share it with them. Yet these people want to visit the castle. They want to have their aristocrats and eat them.

My advice to the newcomer, aristocrat or not, is: be commercial. Be as commercial as you can make it. Here are a few hasty tips about problems and difficulties.

1. Selling souvenirs is, for some reason unfathomable to me, regarded as the uttermost depths of commerciality. Do not be deterred. Just go on selling souvenirs; pictures, prints, ash-trays with crests, plastic animals (with crests or without), books, etc. This *etc* is no empty word. It comprises, in my case, more than five hundred items. The turnover of my souvenir-shops amounts to £180,000 a year. So it is a service to me and will be a service to you; and it is, most definitely, a service to the public too. They are no victims of sharp selling practices: they *want* these souvenirs. To be at Woburn or Shackleton Castle* is nice; to *have been* there is often even nicer. People want the evidence of their visit. Be kind and give it to them.

* This may, or again may not, be the name of your Stately Home.

43

2. Catering is not quite so much beneath one's dignity in certain eyes as selling souvenirs, but is not much better. Once again: do not falter. Just cater. Having no catering facilities is deadly. People – at least some people – will come even so, but they will rush through your rooms at an incredible speed – some doing the mile in under four minutes – and will leave, never to come again. A few proud owners of Stately Homes who have sunk to selling souvenirs and catering feel that they can preserve the last shred of their dignity by keeping their places cold. (Do not misunderstand me: I am not speaking of air-conditioning but of lack of heating in winter.) That may help dignity but does not help business.

3. Do not forget about security. This is a great problem for every place which has something to guard. Ordinary visitors may or may not be interested in art treasures; thieves invariably are. You may say a lot of uncomplimentary things about thieves but they do love beautiful things. For a long time I have been deeply hurt because nothing has ever been stolen from Woburn. Of course, I try to console myself with the thought that our security system is uncommonly good – but can it also be the discriminating thieves don't find us up to scratch? I was only slightly reassured the other day by a woman who was seen in a mirror to conceal a candle-stick under her coat.

One more word about the excellence of our security. It is so efficient that I myself am not authorized to have a key to my house. They say – and not without some justification – that I am a little absent-minded and let

They will rush through your rooms at an incredible speed

How to run a Stately Home

things such as keys lie around. All an efficient thief would have to do would be to pick up my keys, walk in and help himself to a Rembrandt or a Canaletto. So whenever I get home I have to ring the bell and wait. As a rule they open the door and let me in.

4. Even the most obliging and eager-to-please Stately-Home owner cannot satisfy all his customers. I am often criticized for not having added any new cars to my vintage car collection. Others cannot even find my vintage-car collection at all and reproach me bitterly for this. The point is, of course, that they mix me up with the Montagu Motor Museum and blame me for being Woburn Abbey in Bedfordshire not Beaulieu Abbey in Hampshire. When I tell them that this is their mistake, they think it a feeble excuse, quite unworthy of me. For years I have been even more vociferously blamed for not exhibiting my lions. Here the confusion was with Henry Bath's place, Longleat House at Warminster. He had lions, I did not. All the same, I got so fed up with recriminations that now I have my own lions. One does everything one can to oblige one's customers. About the lack of a motor museum I still have to plead guilty.

5. Do not be afraid of strikes . . . strikes in *other* businesses, I mean. Strikers, as a rule, do not know how to spend their extra free time and often visit Stately Homes.

6. Do not be afraid of being old-fashioned. Being old-fashioned is one of your attractions. People are chasing the most recherché, the most up-to-date entertainment all over the world. They go to Turkey and go to Morocco;

On being commercial

they go on safaris and hunt wild boar in Transylvania; they go to have a look at the North Pole and I have just seen an advertisement inviting tourists to enjoy the unexplored jungles of South America. Your Stately Home will not be able to keep them away from such attractions. But people, having camped at the North Pole and having had a lively time in the jungles of South America, may long for some clean, old-fashioned fun and may even feel some slight nostalgia for the eighteenth century. That's where you come in, with a well-equipped, modern Stately Home, with a decent supply of delights preserved from the past.

Look defiant when people call you commercial, or blush — whichever suits your temperament — but stick to your commercial principles. Only too often have I seen where lack of them can lead. People fail; they have to shut down their Stately Home which then becomes a lunatic asylum, a local government educational centre or part of a factory. Not even a factory's central, main building; just a part. The contents of the house go to Christie's or Sotheby's and the former owners move to the Channel Islands where they drink themselves to death. Or else they build a small house on the edge of their former property and go on living in the shadow of their past glory, feeling like martyrs. Now it is supremely satisfying to feel a martyr when you are not really a martyr, but the fate of a real one is truly sad and deserves sympathy. Roots go very deep, people are attached to their old places and it

How to run a Stately Home

hurts to turn the key, close them down for good, and watch them crumble.

Being commercial, I feel, is still the lesser of two evils. And I have one further consolation: people only knock you as long as you are worth knocking. So carry on, knockers.

Why do they come?

I am an expert – if at all – on Stately Homes and not on the human soul, but I like to continue observing people and it strikes me that there are two main reasons – seemingly contradictory – which bring people to places like Woburn. There are a few other uncomplicated – indeed childishly simple – reasons too, and I shall come to those a little later.

The first reason is the desire for *identification*. Some people feel an equally strong desire for non-identification and although this seems contradictory, obviously it is not; it is the same motive with a minus-sign in front of it.

I watched a woman who was looking round one of my rooms which contains about £800,000 worth of stuff. I speak to many people – as many as I can – but I did not speak to her. Somebody else did, however, and I overheard him ask her what she liked most in that room. She answered without a moment's hesitation.

'The lino. I like it very much indeed. It's exactly what I want for my kitchen.'

I was pleased. A Stately Home may not be an Ideal Home but it is comforting to learn that at least some people regard the exhibits as they do those in an Ideal Home Exhibition.

How to run a Stately Home

Another lady examined a number of plates, dishes, vases and bowls made of solid gold. She was quite absorbed in the spectacle. When she looked up she saw me standing by her.

'I do like your brass,' she said. 'What do you clean it with?'

You may (or again may not) have great art treasures, but a fair number of people are only interested in the commonplace things they can see in any home, however un-stately, above all their own. They look with immense interest at your television set and they are much more concerned about its size, its make and whether it is colour or black-and-white than they are about your seventeenth-century embroidery. The Ming dynasty is all right, but what they really want to know is what soap you use and where you bought your curtains and vacuum cleaner. Chippendale break-front book-cases are, they readily accept, quite beautiful but they are more interested in your bathroom for the simple reason that they have no Chippendale break-front book-cases at home but they do have a bathroom.

I say this with approval, not as criticism. I have no reason whatsoever for feeling superior. I have spent a lot of time – year in, year out – studying various aspects of art: paintings, furniture, china and so on. I have always been interested in such things and knowing about them is part of my job. Yet whenever I visit the Victoria and Albert Museum, I leave it with a very uncomfortable feeling, quite appalled at my own ignorance. So why should I

Are only interested in the commonplace things

blame others for not knowing very much about such things – others, whose professional interest lies elsewhere? People look at the simple, everyday things in your house because they want to identify themselves with you, their lives with yours. That is a compliment and should be taken as such. It means that, in spite of all appearances to the contrary, they still regard you as human. Occasionally you wonder if they are right in this kind and friendly supposition, but it is gratifying.

Other visitors come because they are trying to escape into a different world. They lead a humdrum life and they invest the Stately Home with an air of romance which their own home does not possess. Such a visitor wishes to spend some hours in a make-believe world and to become a lord for a day. He chooses the right length of time. I wonder if he would like it if it lasted any longer.

Again, for a large number of people identification is mixed with a good deal of what the Germans call *Schadenfreude* – a useful word lacking in our language. Some writers and linguists maintain that the lack of this word is our great glory, showing what splendid people we are because the sentiment itself – rejoicing at someone else's misfortune – is not a laudable one. Whether the word is missing because we are so magnanimous or because our language is not quite so rich as we like to believe, is beside the point; the point is that even if the word is lacking the feeling is frequently present and I often come across it in a not too unpleasant and quite human form. It's very nice to have these treasures – people seem to say –

Why do they come?

and we are pleased to see them. All the same we are happy that they belong to you and not to us. These people look at your antique furniture and rejoice in their hearts that it is you who have to keep it clean, not they. They look at your silver and they feel happy that they do not have to polish it. They walk on some splendid mosaic floor and ask you what the best cleaning material is for it. They look at your priceless Sèvres porcelain – given by one of the Louis to one of the Dukes of Bedford – and feel overjoyed that it is not they who have to wash it up after a regal but greasy meal.

There are some people who come to see the art treasures and appreciate them as such, with discrimination. I get more than 1,200,000 visitors a year. Of these about 800,000 come to see the Game Park alone, about five hundred are art experts, and a few thousand more are genuinely interested in the arts. I specially enjoy these people's presence, but I do not try to educate my other visitors or force anything down their throats. Swings, slides and roundabouts are things everybody understands and if people want to enjoy those and be happy, I am delighted. Give pleasure to people – that is why you are, or should be, in the Stately Home business, and if you can cater for all tastes, you will do well. A Rembrandt here, a slide there; a Van Dyck here, a Punch and Judy show there. In the end, of course, many people will frown at you, low-brows and high-brows alike. Some will call the slides and roundabouts vulgar, others will only be interested in *them* and will call the paintings high-brow rubbish. All this criticism may be slightly aggravating every now and then but, when you feel irritated, think of the late Mrs Roosevelt's wise advice. As long as you are convinced in the depths of your heart that what you are doing is right and that it does no harm to anyone – indeed, gives pleasure to many – do not mind what people say, just go on doing what you think right.

Others again come simply because your place has become well-known and is included in their guide-books. A number of Dutch or Scottish school-teachers, for instance, may spend three days in these parts and having seen Stratford-upon-Avon and the ballet in London, they will visit your place. Travel agencies may favour you because their clients must have tea *somewhere*, and your Stately Home seems to make as good a stopping place – or perhaps slightly better – as an ordinary tea-shop. Businessmen may come to you to entertain their foreign buyers and colleagues – dine and wine them in your restaurant. Even those who do not care for fifteenth-century Italian paintings may find the surroundings out of the ordinary and fascinating. Not a bad place to clinch a deal. Many will find that your Stately Home is not a bad place for a wedding reception. Or a group of three hundred Americans, before going to a theatre in London, will come down for tea and a look round the antique market. (Some of the buyers – a few among so many – are bound to be phonies; take the utmost care that all the antiques offered for sale are genuine.)

All should be made welcome, even those people – quite

Why do they come?

a number of them – who come to you just to knock the place. Many of these are genuine art-lovers, but not the nicest and most lovable of that breed. The main purpose of their journey is to scrutinize your furniture, or china, or silver, or paintings, then tell you that they have seen something much better elsewhere. One of them explained to me that my Guardis, while undoubtedly genuine, were the poorest Guardis he had ever seen. What could I reply? I pointed out that I had no Guardis at all, excellent or poor, but I doubt if such a feeble argument carried any weight with him. Another man travelled quite a long distance in order to point out to me that one of my Rembrandts was a fake. It was painted by Rembrandt himself for one of my ancestors. Had this gentleman been present when Rembrandt handed over the picture to my great-great-great-grandfather he would, no doubt, have pointed out that Rembrandt himself was a fake. But if some people take pleasure in deriding your exhibits and calling your paintings fakes – well, they, too are customers and they too want to enjoy themselves in their own way, so allow them to do so.

And then the day will come when you will ask yourself whether there is any virtue in it all? Of course, it is easy to praise oneself – most of us are inclined to be kinder to ourselves than we are to other people – and to rate one's work high. After all, those of us who are in this business – do we not give high aesthetic pleasure to many people? Do we not preserve works of art and beautiful buildings for posterity? It is easy to say all this at much greater length and in more high-flown language. But I do have my doubts about posterity. After all, *we* are posterity, too. Ask the Romans or even the Victorians. We are not so much wiser and more appreciative than our predecessors were, so why expect *our* posterity to be wiser and more appreciative than we are? I personally am not much concerned about posterity but I do care about the present; I like the people around me and I also like the beautiful things my house contains.

You, on the other hand, may feel yourself justified by the service you are doing for posterity, and you are welcome to do so. It is little more, really, than a question of phraseology. We Stately Home owners are all trying to do the same thing. Some of us speak of posterity; others of business. But we all have the same thing in mind. I like to think that my children and grandchildren will continue to preserve Woburn; that my work has not been in vain; but of course it is up to them to make the decision.

Dinner with a Duke

An American lady had a good look at Rembrandt's self-portrait. She examined it thoroughly and for a long time. Then she turned to me and asked: 'And where is the original?'

But I have heard much worse than that. I think the unbeatable remark was made by a lady – well-dressed and well-spoken – who, having wandered through all my rooms and having observed all my Old Masters most attentively, came up to me and remarked, with true admiration in her voice: 'It must have taken an awful lot of time for you to paint all these pictures.'

She had a point, in a way. Had I painted all my pictures it would, undoubtedly, have taken a lot of time, and her remark has often been a great comfort to me. Whenever I think of all the time I saved by *not* painting all my pictures, my heart rejoices.

More and more people arrive from Europe and I always have a fair number from the Commonwealth, but most of my non-British visitors are Americans. They like coming to Britain and they are most welcome. Whether we have a special relationship between our Heads of State or not, there is certainly one between our ordinary people, and the average American tourist feels more closely linked with us than, say, the average Ghanaian tourist, although it's the latter who is a member of the Commonwealth. Whatever the Americans have now is theirs alone; but our *heritage* is common.

Many Americans come here in search of ancestors. Tracing American ancestors, I am told, is a budding industry, becoming quite big business, so if your Stately Home gets off to a disappointing start and you feel the need for a side-line, I suggest that you go into the ancestor business. A great many Americans *do* have Anglo-Saxon ancestors, so the search – alas – often has to be genuine. I say *alas* because this means hard work: you must be extremely conscientious, visit many places, examine many documents. These genuine people will give you a lot of trouble, so avoid them if you can. The clients you should go after are Americans of, for instance, Sicilian or Lebanese descent, particularly those who have a lot of money. You may think at first that in these cases the ancestor-search will take quite a time, but second thoughts will no doubt make it clear that the supply of ancestors for people in this category lies near at hand and is limitless (unless you have a very uninventive mind). It is worth keeping in mind that people are prepared to pay about fifteen to twenty per cent more for Scottish ancestors than for English ones.

For the people of Anglo-Saxon descent you are performing a genuine service in adding a few generations to their family tree. They will be grateful, and will express

Dinner with a Duke

their gratitude in a concrete and realistic manner. Particularly if you prove that their ancestors sailed on the *Mayflower*. The *Mayflower* was a huge vessel and arrived with about 50,000 people on board; during the journey, I am told, many passengers complained bitterly to the Captain that the ship lacked air-conditioning.

Many Americans come to Woburn, and a large number spend a night there. Some American magazines described this facility – not too subtly, I admit, but the wording was not mine – as 'Dinner with a Duke!' This Dinner with a Duke idea has been discussed quite a bit. Some smiled at the Americans and others, as usual, derided me for conducting my business in such a blatant manner. But this is a very straightforward operation which gives me great pleasure (and, yes, some profit; I never said I was a charitable organization). It also, I know, gives some pleasure to my guests as well. I recommend the operation to beginners, and this is how it works.

First, it is not true, as I have heard alleged many times, that vast agencies are at work to get customers for me. No agencies are at work at all, vast or tiny. I get all the necessary publicity, free of charge, through American television and radio because people become genuinely interested. Then, either through travel agents or directly, they get in touch with me and ask for an invitation.

People who ask for invitations are vetted, which serves two purposes, one for the host and one for the guest. If you are having people to stay in your house you must know who they are so that you can judge whether the visit will

How to run a Stately Home

be agreeable both to you and to them. From the guests' point of view, the possibility of rejection (which does, of course, really exist) makes acceptance all the more gratifying. Receiving your invitation counts as a sort of social recognition; you have succeeded in joining a club where not everyone can become a member. Sometimes I feel that the rare occasions when we have turned someone down are as good publicity as any TV show. But do not think me more cynical than I am: the first and main purpose of the vetting remains the obvious one, which is that of letting me know to whom I am offering hospitality.

Selection is not made on a money basis and has nothing to do with what some people would call social distinction. Anyone whom I (or rather my wife) feel would fit in is welcome, whether he has money or not. There is an Austrian hairdresser who has stayed with me three times and who I will be glad to see again; there is a well-known business tycoon who has been rejected. Come to think of it, that is not a very good example, since nowadays hairdressers tend to be richer than tycoons, but the fact remains that my guests are not chosen for their millions. As Mr Justice Darling once said: British justice is open to rich and poor alike, just like the Ritz Hotel. Anyone who can pay my not unreasonable but not inconsiderable fee of about £90 a night, all inclusive, may be as poor as a church-mouse but will still be received with open arms, if he is otherwise acceptable.

My guests are a cross-section of the population of many lands, and in fact quite a few of them are not particularly

Dinner with a Duke

well-off. I often get school-teachers and others involved in education or the arts. This visit is something rather different from other tourist attractions and I strongly advise you to introduce it into your Stately Home. You will enjoy the procedure as much as your guests do.

Well, what actually happens? A party consists of four, six, or a maximum of eight people. My guests arrive in the afternoon. They are taken to their rooms (complete with bathrooms of course, and one or two minor masterpieces on the wall). When they come down to my library – in the private section of my house, not open to the public, and containing my collection of self-portraits – we have a good traditional English tea, complete with scones and crumpets. After tea I drive them round the park which consists of three thousand acres, so it is quite a drive. Sometimes, when we are a party of eight, my wife comes with us and we use two cars. We visit the Game Park, meet the lions, giraffes, zebras and monkeys (more about them later). Then we return to the library where we have a few drinks.

Then they go up to their rooms where the valet has, in the meantime, unpacked their suitcases, laid ready the necessary garments and run a bath. More often than not, black ties are worn for dinner; occasionally the dress is more informal. When I have my own dinner, after a particularly heavy day, eating cold pork pie from a tray, I hardly ever change into a dinner jacket; but for such an occasion it is the correct garment and my guests prefer it, too.

How to run a Stately Home

Dinner is at eight. Having made the necessary inquiries well in advance, we know who our guests are and what their background is and can invite those of our local or London friends who will provide the most congenial company for them. Teachers or university professors will meet English teachers and English dons; businessmen will meet English businessmen and bankers English bankers. I want them to feel they are my personal guests because that is exactly what they are.

The dinner is very good indeed, cooked by an excellent French chef who was trained by my excellent French wife, and is accompanied by a good selection of wines and champagne. The dining-room contains my twenty-four Canalettos and is open to the public for a small extra fee. At lunchtime I sometimes have to hurry with my meal because the public is due to arrive, and watching me eat my lunch is not part of the bargain, but in the evenings there is no public around any longer. After dinner we go back to the library.

After coffee and liqueurs we make a tour of the house. It is beautifully lit and eighteenth-century music is relayed throughout. I point out the various pieces of interest and the tour lasts about an hour and a half. By 11 or 11.30 we are back in the library for more drinks, and we go to bed at about midnight.

Next morning my guests are served a real old-fashioned English breakfast in bed and then depart without seeing me again. I think they must like it because many of them return. A few come back again and again.

Special people with special requests

How to run a Stately Home

I have been accused by some cynical observers of deliberately tiring my guests during our after-dinner tour so that they will go to bed early. I do tire them out, but not deliberately; such tours *are* tiring. Even so, as I have said, we stay up till midnight or so, and that is late enough for most people. Admittedly, it is usually late enough for me.

Sometimes we make special arrangements for special people with special requests. There was one American school-teacher, for example, who wanted to spend three days with us. We provided a special programme for her lasting three days: we did all the usual things and in addition we took her to Stratford, to the ballet in London and to a night-club in Berkeley Square.

The main thing is: do it for your guests' sake and enjoy it yourself. If you don't, it won't be any good. And you must, of course, be present. 'Dinner with a Duke' without the Duke is just not the genuine article.

The circuit

For a long time there were jocular remarks in the gossip columns, in clubs and during society dinners about this 'Dinner with a Duke' gimmick of mine (*they* called it a gimmick, not I). Slowly, however, more and more of the jokers followed my lead. They all started taking energetic steps to get on to this Dinner with a Duke circuit, and as soon as you open your Stately Home you should do the same.

I have just seen the catalogue of a Texas department store which offers the ultimate in tours of elegance and distinction. 'The ultimate of European tours, twenty-two days of sheer luxury as guests of the aristocracy. Like the Royal Progress that Tudor Kings and Queens made through their realm, nothing is spared. They will be entertained by Dukes, Earls, Marquises and Princes, chauffeured from castle to stately home in limousines with personal maids or valets and hairdressers at almost every stop. Romantics will love it. They will feel they are living in a novel or movie. The gregarious will have a wonderful time with the most interesting people in the world.'

The prices are not moderate but what do you expect if

How to run a Stately Home

you want to meet 'the most interesting people in the world' (that's you and me)? To the uninitiated reader it is not quite clear who is keener on meeting whom: the transAtlantic public on meeting us – Dukes, Marquises, Princes, etc – or the Dukes, Marquises and Princes on meeting these modern Tudor Kings and Queens, the American tourists.

This development is not unexpected, at least by me. I have been watching the development of travel-mania for a long time and have been studying it with keen selfish and unselfish interest. For long years new and unexpected holiday places were constantly being discovered by the intellectuals and the snobs; places 'off the beaten track', known only to the most knowledgeable and most distinguished. It was not so long ago that even Ibiza was an isolated place, known only to the initiated. Then the crowd followed and the select few moved on. Remote Greek islands with permanent howling gales, and desolate villages in Asia Minor where the scorching sun burned holes in your skin, became popular resorts. Then even the most ingenious snobs started running out of ideas. There were not enough places on the globe. They were reduced, despairingly, to rediscovering old favourites. People had almost forgotten the words 'French Riviera' because it was so long since anyone who was anyone had dared to utter them – one of the best holiday-grounds of Europe had remained unmentionable in informed circles for years – but now someone has had the brilliant idea of rediscovering the French Riviera. No one actually *boasts* of

The circuit

going there, and they tend to disguise it by referring only to the name of the resort or village where they stay ('a little place not far from St Trop'), but the French Riviera is what they mean, and very nice too. They look a bit sheepish but they enjoy themselves.

In this atmosphere British Stately Homes were bound to be discovered and if you, too, want to have a share in the boom of the Texan Tudors, now is the time to join in. Competition is keen. Burke's peerage has many thousands of names in it and Debrett contains well over three thousand pages. One Piccadilly travel agent alone offers you a choice of three hundred aristocratic hosts. Some are named: two days and nights with a certain Viscount costs £88. Others remain anonymous but skilful pen-sketches make them more than faintly recognizable.

'Your Host was born in 1923, was educated at Eton, and served in the Coldstream Guards during the war. He is an expert skin-diver and speaks a little French and Italian.' Or: 'Your Hostess is the daughter of a retired Army officer, and loves water-skiing and interior decorating. She owns a boutique in Bath. Your hosts have three sons.' The quotes come from Michael Bateman's Atticus column in the *Sunday Times*.

I have already referred to the famous and much advertised department store in Texas where, it is said, you are not allowed even to window shop unless you possess at least two million dollars. They, needless to say, must do a little better than others. Their brochure points out that they cannot possibly mention names: 'Society at this level has its own protocol. There are those who accepted party invitations *so* close to Royalty that their names must not be published.'

The brochure does not actually say so, but it goes as near as possible to saying that with a little more financial pressure from Texas Buckingham Palace itself might be turned into a Stately Home, offering bed and breakfast to carefully selected tourists provided they can afford the price. Well, we have not quite reached that stage yet, but you must be convinced by now that competition in this field is pretty stiff even if not quite so stiff as the Texan store hints.

And as if competition among Stately Homes were not enough, the most unstately come in, too. Of course, most tourists want to drive from Stately Home to Stately Home, from Dukes to Marquises, chauffeured by Knights of the Garter and Princes, enjoying the sparkling conversation of 'the most interesting people in the world' and stopping at hairdressers by the way who – for a few extra pounds – build you a newly-invented hairstyle, called 'The Aristocrat'. But they also want to meet 'the real people of England'. So an odd visit or two to pubs in the East End and Dagenham are thrown in where 'the real people of England' are known to congregate.

I always thought that I, too, was a real person, in the sense that I, too, belonged to the human race. This supposition is denied by some, who feel that I have not quite made it, while others maintain that being a Duke I must be *super*human. Be that as it may, I have the vague feeling –

Being a Duke I must be superhuman

How run to a Stately Home

perhaps unjustified – that when guests come to stay with me I manage to remain almost human. But I wonder what those other 'real people' make of it when a few dozen American tourists invade their pubs and insist on meeting them on a chummy man-to-man basis. I should not be surprised if their manners did not remain utterly relaxed and if they tended to become, at such moments, as characteristic of everyday life in England as are Westminster Abbey or Nelson's Column.

The Commonwealth

English-speaking non-American and non-British visitors form a special class. They want to belong; and, of course, they do belong. They care little for the swings or the roundabouts; they are not interested in the price or value of things; they do pay a visit to the Game Park but lions and zebras, too, are only of secondary interest to them. What fascinates them is history and tradition. They want to know all about the house, a lot about the Russells, the Earls and Dukes of Bedford, the part the house played during the Civil War, Queen Victoria's visit and all the details. Such visits are part and parcel of the England they have come to visit and confirm their sense of being rooted in its past.

I find this reverent interest in Englishness rather comforting nowadays, when mourning our decline has become such a fashionable pastime. One is reminded, to one's surprise, that we do have a few features which other people still see as enviable and would like to have themselves. Daisies, for example. One lady from a more arid part of the Commonwealth was seen digging up a daisy plant in the park and carefully putting it into a little plastic bag: she was going to smuggle it home, she said,

They are interested in history and tradition

so that her garden should boast a genuine English daisy. And a gentleman from an Australian group considered making me an offer for my Rembrandt self-portrait and asked me how much I wanted for it. He thought it was a nice idea, he told me, to take a Rembrandt back to Australia. But another member of his group told him that all such things were superfluous.

'Don't bother, Jack,' he said. 'We already have a Rembrandt in Australia.'

The Europeans

The Europeans are quite a different kettle of fish. They are not interested in tradition or in common heritage. They believe – and I often wonder whether they are right or wrong – that we British are far from being Europeans, and hold no heritage in common with them at all. They do not care for our history and know very little about it. In any case, they look at it from a very different angle.

A friend once told me that his son had to be educated in France (where the family were living) but he was a little worried about the way in which the French taught history. They are utterly biased, he told his son. The son – more French by then than the most patriotic Frenchman – protested strongly and said that, on the contrary, it was the English who distorted history and taught it with tremendous bias, thereby misleading poor innocent English boys. The dispute had become heated when the father asked his son: 'Very well. Tell me then, for instance, what have you learnt about Trafalgar?'

The boy replied in a flash: 'The truth. That it was an inconclusive sea-battle in which a British Admiral lost his life.'

Yes, the Europeans come with a different outlook. For

them we are the bizarre and eccentric English. Dukes, Stately Homes, the aristocracy, our rituals, our dress, our manners are all part of the crazy English system. They come to laugh at us, or at the very least – the kinder among them – to enjoy a peculiar show: the strange and incredible Englishman in his own castle. No English home is less of a castle than a castle open to the public, of course. (This is not a complaint – I am simply pointing out that they come to see the wrong things.) But that is what they want to see: the Stately Home comes under the same heading as the top-hatted bank-messengers of the City, the changing of the guard, trooping the colour, the mace, the bewigged judges and the Tower where, unfortunately, beheadings have become rather few and far between and are not included in the entrance fee. I wonder how our joining the Common Market will affect their attitude, and ours. Will Europe gradually absorb us, making us more European and less eccentric every year? There are those who answer no, Europeans will discover that they have joined Britain rather than the other way round; but native modesty prevents me from counting on this – and besides, I would deplore any development which ironed out the differences which give so much innocent amusement to my European visitors.

They have one very good quality, though. They hardly ever complain while here and never, or hardly ever, write letters telling you off. It is true that often there are linguistic difficulties. If you cannot speak or write English, it is a little more difficult to complain. But many of them,

To enjoy a peculiar show

of course, speak fluent, even excellent English and they could grumble if they wanted to. Some come from faraway countries where democracy has less strong roots and grumbling is not such a national pastime as here; but others come from countries every bit as democratic as ours, yet they too refrain from grumbling or complaint.

They just come, look around and laugh at us. When they arrive they already have a strong suspicion that we must not be taken seriously; when they leave, they *know*.

Entrance fee

I must also draw your attention to a different species. He belongs to no nationality and all nationalities.

He is a very rich man who refuses to pay the entrance fee. This is not because he finds 25 new pence excessive (although the mysteries of human nature are unfathomable and you never know). It probably has more to do with pride than with avarice.

I knew a man during the war who gave huge house parties under the most difficult circumstances. Food was scarce and rationed in those days, and he had to go to tremendous trouble and expense to keep his house parties going. But he would go to any length to achieve this, and no trouble and no expense were too great for him. He was a truly generous host and his guests appreciated this quality in him. Yet every night (on Saturdays *and* Sundays) people had to sit down and play rummy or canasta with him. He played both games very badly but he *had* to win. It was a necessity which bolstered his ego. So he cheated like hell. He cheated not only recklessly but also clumsily. All his guests knew that he was cheating; he knew that they knew, yet he could not help it. He was modest, indeed his modesty was touching. He was satisfied with a win of half-a-crown, five shillings at the most. In order to gain his weekly five bob he was delighted to spend a weekly fifty pounds.

In his case money was obviously not the driving force, and our non-payers, as I have said, may also be motivated by complex feelings. Nevertheless, the truth remains that there are multimillionaires who do not think twice before spending huge sums on anything you care to mention, who absolutely refuse to pay 25 new pence entrance fee and will go to ridiculous lengths to avoid that indignity. The richer they are, the more reluctant they will be to pay. A man with a small fortune not exceeding twenty-five million dollars might, perhaps, pay the entrance fee, however reluctantly. Anyone with over twenty-five million will not even contemplate it.

They will write to you from distant parts of the world, telling you that they are coming. The hint is always quite clear: they want to be invited. Not for lunch; not for dinner; not to stay with you. Just to enter the place free of charge. Anyone who owns an art gallery in Ohio, a Manet in Nebraska or has seen several Tintorettos in his youth in Bogota, feels that he belongs to the freemasonry of the art world and must be let in free of charge.

A certain number of these people are complete phoneys, and some of them are burglars. The burglar wants to get into your confidence so that he can see the really good and valuable stuff. A large number of burglars are known to have joined art societies and societies specializing in old china or jewellery. They are the cream of their profession and are interested only in the cream of art treasures.

They try to find out which picture is my favourite

How to run a Stately Home

If I get a letter nowadays from a very distinguished but unknown luminary, I check up on him. Not so long ago I received a letter written on the most elegant and expensive writing paper I have ever seen. It came from a Duc de . . . He had a double-barrelled name, one more famous and distinguished than the other. The whole thing looked a little too good to be true. My wife, a Frenchwoman herself, had never heard of this distinguished Frenchman. So I rang up the wife of the French Ambassador who told me that both of the families mentioned on the writing paper died out in the fifteenth century. So I failed to respond.

About two weeks later a very valuable painting was stolen from a Stately Home. The thief was the Duc de . . . I showed the police the elegant letter I had received; the victim of the theft had had a similar one. The police checked on the address given by the Duc: it was a phoney one, used as a forwarding address for about two weeks.

Criminals are, however, a tiny minority. The real snobs who try to avoid paying are quite harmless. As a rule they insist on seeing me. As I am readily available to all, this is not difficult. They try to find out which picture is my favourite. Once told, they assure me that it is a fake and not even a good one.

They need to do this for the happiness of their souls. As I am a basically good-natured man, I am prepared to nod assent and let them enjoy themselves all the more: a small price to pay for a fellow human being's mental equilibrium.

Entrance fee

Although once, I must admit, I couldn't help flinching. One of these visitors persuaded me to show him a specially valuable and much cherished china service of mine. He examined a few pieces carefully, then nodded: 'Yes. That's the same as the Arpad Plesches use for their picnics.'

Against Stately Homes

Before you embark upon opening your old Stately Home to the public or on buying a new one, I ought to warn you that if you do this you will be going against the modern trend.

I often wonder what is going to be left of the new, modern fortunes. The answer is: *nothing*. Or not much. Our ancestors, when they had money, built huge houses, castles and palaces. They were often ugly, even hideous; they were often ridiculously large, cold and uncomfortable. But they were *there*, to be seen, to hit posterity in the eye.

Today men do not build on that scale. I cannot say that the arts are forgotten because people are still buying pictures. Indeed, buying pictures has become a mania. But today few people buy pictures because they like pictures, understand pictures and want to be surrounded by pictures. Today people buy pictures as an *investment* – as people in less sophisticated but more attractive ages bought gold bullion, shares or gilt-edged securities. Today Picasso replaces the bullion, Matisse the tobacco shares and Renoir the consols. Very rich people have a lot of pictures but they do not know where to put them.

How to run a Stately Home

(It is unjust to say that the new rich buy pictures *only* for investment. Sometimes they have more practical and immediate purposes. I know a gentleman who employed an interior decorator to furnish his beautiful new country house. The decorator was satisfied with his work—so was the owner—but he found that one wall in the dining-room was too bare. He told the owner that all was well except for that single wall which needed something to cover its nudity but he had no idea at the moment what. The gentleman himself had a simple idea: he went to an art dealer and bought £320,000 worth of Impressionist paintings. The wall is now covered, which proves that you can solve any problem with a little goodwill and ingenuity.)

So the New Rich have the paintings but (with exceptions such as the above) they do not know where to hang them. The modern New Rich have no Big Places and that is why I want to warn everybody to think twice before going into the Stately Home business. It is a bit out of fashion.

Today one buys *many small places*. The modern rich man will have a house in London and one or two in the country; he will have a flat in Paris; one in Rome; a place in the mountains; another on the sea. He will need a skiing place; he will need a yacht or two – otherwise how can he show his face? The modern rich man has many tiny places, all looking like so many hotel rooms. Some have as many as twenty places scattered over Europe, over the world. A lot of stuff will be packed into them, often good, valuable

Twenty places all over Europe, all over the world

and beautiful things but they will not be properly hung and will give pleasure to no one. Stacked up in the way they are, they are no more beautiful than a pack of shares used to be, locked up in a safe.

The other strong tendency of the day is not to show off with your wealth. This is prompted not by modesty but by prudence. You do not wish to arouse the interest of the tax-man. On the other hand human nature has not changed – and certainly not for the better – so the desire to show off remains at the bottom of most hearts. But how can you have your cake and eat it? Obviously, you must choose ways and means which will impress your fellow men but will not provoke the income-tax inspector to descend upon you with extra fury.

Many people have great collections and keep very quiet about them. Great collections have the extra advantage of holding their value – indeed, growing in value – but not bringing in any income that might interest the tax-man. I heard of a lady who had bought a pair of earrings for £200,000, but did not dare to wear them. Perhaps the knowledge that she *has* a pair of earrings much too valuable to be worn and much too precious to show to the *hoi polloi* (and the tax people) gives her a special new type of satisfaction.

People do buy flashy cars, but the tax inspector does not actually *see* anyone's car. Otherwise even the most ostentatious and the most vulgar member of the New Rich is torn between the two instincts, to show off and to hide his money. The modern rich live seemingly simple lives

Against Stately Homes

at many places. Space was the mark of old riches: huge houses, palaces and parks; *mobility* is the hallmark of new riches. The newly rich man will buy a private jet; he will buy no palaces. He will buy expensive pictures to cover his walls but as soon as they are hung he flies away in his private jet. It never occurs to him to stay in his house to admire the pictures.

If some of the new rich were inclined to behave like the old rich (who were new rich once too) their wives would disapprove. The big place means a lot of responsibility and who wants responsibility? The big place needs a large staff and women know only too well how difficult it is to get staff, even Turkish and Portuguese staff. But they know something else too, and something very important. They know that a large staff transforms them into a member of that very same staff. A wife may be the head of the staff, its supervisor and general, yet she becomes part of it, she has to be bothered with problems of cleaning and cooking. The modern woman has discovered to her surprise and dismay that she is not the mistress of the Big House any more, just a glorified housekeeper, and this notion does not please her. She prefers to stay in small houses, even service flats, luxury hotels and sea-side bungalows hired on a weekly basis. She prefers any situation where she is being looked after instead of looking after others.

On food

Libraries have been written about 'Food and the English' and quite a few volumes could be added on 'Food in Stately Homes'. The British Food Revolution preceded the British Sex Revolution by about ten years. It was then that it was discovered that food *could* be enjoyable; that it was only one of the minor puritanical virtues to eat food only for nourishment to keep body and soul together; that you might actually *enjoy* food and still remain a decent, patriotic Englishman.

The trouble in the early days, in fact, went even deeper. Many of us thought that the British were eating that washed-out cabbage cooked in salt water because they refused to enjoy their food. I am driven to the conclusion – sad as it may seem – that they were just as hedonistic about their food as the French. The melancholy truth is that the British enjoyed that soggy cabbage as much as the French enjoyed the masterpieces of their cuisine – and certainly much more than they, the British, would enjoy the masterpieces of the French cuisine. In those days they thought that cottage pie and steak and kidney pud were the most delicious dishes in the world (and they can, I admit, taste pretty good when properly made) and that the French did not have the faintest idea how to eat or what to eat. I met once a young girl, the daughter of a plumber, who ventured over to France with a girl-friend in the early fifties. It was brave of her to go and intelligent of her to want to go at all. She enjoyed every minute of her journey and decided to go abroad as often as she could. 'Everything was wonderful in France,' she told me with a conspiratorial, funny grimace, 'except the food.' The idea was, of course, that it was understood between us that while the French were nice, interesting and quite worthy people, there was one thing they ought to learn from us: how to cook decent food.

A lot of things have happened since those early days of the British Food Revolution. Millions of Britons have been abroad and have gradually become persuaded that some foreigners, particularly the French, know a thing or two about cooking. They have learnt so much that while many of them have remained – quite rightly – fond of their own national dishes, they now realize that even steak and kidney pie, Lancashire hotpot and the rest of it have to be prepared nowadays with greater care and skill than in the pre-revolutionary days.

The improvement has been slow and painful. Admittedly, gone are the days when you were unable to get a good meal in London. Some people still maintain that a British *Good Food Guide* should contain one solitary sentence, 'Cross the Channel', but they are unfair and wrong. You *can* eat excellent meals on all levels – cheap, medium priced and murderously expensive – not only in

On food

London but also in the provinces (in fact, even more in the provinces) so long as you know where to go. In France, if you choose your restaurant at random and drop into any odd place, you have a greater chance of success but the point is that you *can* eat eat very well in England if you know where to go.

By the way, I happen to believe that our food and our climate have a great deal in common, and not only because two such important factors quite obviously must be strong character-forming influences. I see a strange parallel between the two.

Our weather is the subject of the oldest of old jokes, even the most humourless bores have a few facetious stock remarks on the subject. Everybody knows that our weather is rotten and the weather, say, in Northern Italy or on the Riviera is wonderful. If we have seven successive beautiful summers here and they have seven awful summers over there, this will not make the slightest difference to the general belief. Here everyone will say: 'Not a bad summer. Most unusual for our wretched climate.' Over there: 'What a rotten summer. Most unusual for us, we always have glorious weather here.' And the reputation of both regions will go on unchanged. But the truth is that while we often have wretched *weather* here our *climate* is very good indeed. We may get soaked more often than we like, but the general effect of the climate is most beneficial if not exactly invigorating: it is hardly ever too cold, hardly ever too hot. The climate is inducive to hard work (I do not say that we take full advantage of

How to run a Stately Home

this allurement but it *is* inducive), or if someone is more inclined to walk, play golf or watch football matches than to work, our climate will suit his convenience, too. Similarly, our individual dishes may not rival the three-star cuisine of the best French restaurants but our *food* – the general intake, the sum total of the things we eat – has a good effect on us. It is healthy; it keeps us fit; it keeps us, on the whole, slim; it causes fewer stomach troubles than almost anywhere in the world. Until recently you had to add: 'But you must forget about the taste.' Today you may remember even the taste.

When you open your own Stately Home, pay the greatest attention to food. I have already described the overwhelming importance of teas and I draw attention to them once again. Other meals are equally important. More people will come to visit your Stately Home because of your good steaks than because of your good Velasquezes.

As my wife is French she was not at first exactly addicted to the English culinary art. She is not quite an addict today, either, but admits to a certain improvement. It saddened her heart in our early public days that we had to feed people in the English style and she refused to have anything to do with the matter. I vaguely suggested that we should run our own restaurants but she would not hear of it.

Then some crisis developed and we had no choice: she had to take over, which she did with heroic determination. She is a good administrator and that she organized things

On food

most efficiently was no surprise to me. But I was a shade more sceptical when she declared that she hated bad food and only good food would be served in our restaurants. I frowned; I smiled inwardly; I waited.

We had an excellent chef at home who had been with us for four years. He had been imported from a neighbouring land but it was not France; it was Eire. He was a master of his art and he was moved over to the public restaurants to supervise the feeding of our visitors. The decision was a wise one. I do not say that everyone immediately appreciated the improvement. Quite a few people would have preferred soggy cabbage cooked in stale salt water; but it slowly dawned on our visitors that good food was preferable to uneatable muck.

Today we have several restaurants on various price-levels, cater for the well-off and the poorer, cater for parties, weddings, company outings, etc, serve several hundred meals a day. Sometimes we open up the Gallery where we can feed three hundred and fifty people.

The other day, quite recently, a coach-driver came into the kitchen of one of our restaurants looking rather lost. In fact he was lost. He had lost his way and was not sure where he had landed. We told him, and he then complained that he and his party were terribly hungry. It was four o'clock in the afternoon, no meal-time in England. My wife improvised a meal for eighty people within a quarter of an hour. If they had insisted on a dinner-dance for two hundred that, I am afraid, would have needed half an hour's preparation.

Cater for the well-off and the poorer

On food

My wife is now dedicated to secretly educating the English. They do not really mind good food so long as the improvement is gradual and they are not shocked by some outlandish innovation. They do not mind eating well so long as they do not *notice* how good the food is. Let them get used to it gradually and they will grow fond of it. The English nowadays fancy themselves as great wine-experts, too. In fact, wine snobbery is a much more developed art here than in France. The French have drunk wine from time immemorial, so to them there is nothing distinguished about wine-drinking. They would never use expressions like 'dining and wining'; *dining* includes *wining* as naturally as it includes chewing. There are no strict rules over there that you must die rather than drink red wine with fish. It depends on the red wine, on the fish and on your mood. But the French – or most of them – can tell good wine from bad, whatever the label may say, and my wife decided that at our place people are going to have good wine, whether they like it or not. And, amazingly enough, they do like it and most of them admit – however grudgingly – that good wine is preferable to undrinkable stuff.

My wife has suffered total and unmitigated defeat only on one front. She told me once, with stern determination: 'There will be no fish and chips at our place!'

That was a somewhat naïve vow and, soon enough, she saw the error of her ways. You just cannot run certain types of British restaurants without fish and chips. You can run a bookshop without books (in fact stationery articles tend to squeeze out the books from bookshops as it is), you can run a bank or an insurance company without money, but you cannot run a place for the British working man without fish and chips. So my wife acknowledged defeat and bowed to public demand. But her defeat was not total and unmitigated, after all. One day she confessed to me in great confidence, hoping that the news would not get round: 'I do give them fish and chips; but I give them *much better* fish and chips than they realize.'

Household problems

If you have a two-roomed flat in a city, you will have problems about how to keep it properly clean. What about your Stately Home?

You will not find it any easier. Here again, my advice is: run a huge place. A large place will impress with its size, whatever its condition. I have one particular Stately Home in mind – and my strong sense of fairness forbids me to name it – which is really nothing more than a huge, ugly, empty shell. Yet, it is doing well, just because of its enormous size. When you try to sort out your cleaning problems you will find that a small Stately Home is even more difficult to keep clean than a small flat or house. After all, you can clean your small flat yourself, but you cannot clean your own Stately Home, however small, because you would have no time left for anything else. Besides, it does not make a good impression on the visitors if they observe you with duster and broom in hand: they expect you to lead the grand life. But as soon as your house is a large one, many of these problems solve themselves.

Not quite, however, and not too easily. You will have to help towards finding a solution and you'll need a

How to run a Stately Home

certain amount of luck. But the position is easier. You will need a lot of cleaning women but it is easier to get a lot than just one or two. The simple reason for this is that the work is less boring in company than in solitude. When three or four women clean the same huge room together, they can chat, gossip, sing, giggle and they are welcome to do so. They will not work less efficiently; they will work better.

They can chat, gossip, sing, giggle

Household problems

As your Stately Home is unlikely to stand in the middle of a High Street, you will have to see to it that the women are brought to you and taken home again. In my case a little bus collects them every morning and takes them home later, either after lunch or in the late afternoon.

A large Stately Home can afford to employ a large staff, a small one cannot. During frequent labour shortages small Stately Homes will start to deteriorate and that is fatal. Once the rot sets in, it is very difficult to stop it. Things will start looking shabby and very unstately. A small house is like a small theatre: it can be very charming, very intimate but it just will not pay.

Not that all large Stately Homes are clean. They could be but they are not. I visited the above mentioned (but unnamed) huge Stately Home and was very taken aback by its lack of cleanliness. I went as an ordinary visitor, paid my entrance fee and was given, at the end of the tour, the visitors' book to sign. I wrote: 'Woburn Abbey is better. And much cleaner.' Perhaps it was not the most tactful thing to say. But it was the most truthful.

When we discuss the problem of cleaning with people, they often ask me whether the women are impressed by the fact that they are cleaning a famous house, whether they associate themselves with its glory and feel they are part of its grandeur. I do not think that it works that way. Our cleaning women – and many of them have been with us for several years – are nice and reliable but they are much less snobbish than the middle class. Or, perhaps it would be safer to say, I know less about *their* type of

How to run a Stately Home

snobbishness which is complicated and moves on different levels. I am sure they are not terribly impressed by the fact that they are cleaning Woburn Abbey (and I can see no reason why they should be). But quite a few people remark: 'This is the cleanest Stately Home in the country.' The cleaners are pleased to hear this and they associate themselves with the place on those grounds. This makes them feel they belong. They feel some pride, they feel loyal. This feeling is very old-fashioned and out of date. The general idea in present-day Britain seems to be that if a job is worth doing, it is worth doing badly.

If you run a Stately Home you will probably have to buy more meat and vegetables than an ordinary household, since your restaurants, cafés, etc naturally require more food-stuff than even the largest family. A more peculiar type of shopping is necessary when you run a zoo. It is not customary for the ordinary householder to go out and spend £40,000 on shopping for white rhinoceroses.

Run a zoo by all means (more of that later) but do not despair: you do not need to become an expert on lions, camels, seals and apes. I know no more about wild animals than before, although I see more of them and we meet regularly. All my animals are leased from a large firm which looks after them, brings them to me, takes them away, services them and renews spare parts when necessary.

At the beginning I felt slightly embarrassed about this. When you think of lions there are a few adjectives which spring readily to mind: proud, brave, ferocious, man-

Household problems

eating, invincible – things like that. *Leased* is not one of the adjectives you naturally connect with the King of Beasts. Yet, all my lions are leased lions. Luckily this does not show. And their roars are genuine.

On ghosts

One absolutely indispensable attraction in your Stately Home is a ghost. All things eerie, frightening and sinister are good for business. If your house has a long and infamous history, it will help; if one or two people were beheaded in the front garden or hanged from the battlements – however long ago – it is welcome. If a gruesome and most foul murder has been committed under your roof, you are lucky. Even if a high-class tart once lived there, it is beneficial; if she later became a Duchess (as was customary in the Restoration) it is better still.

All such things help; but you just cannot do without a ghost. A castle can remain a castle without a drawbridge or a moat; but not without a ghost.

Woburn Abbey has its ghost but I am sorry to confess that it's not a very good specimen. Alas, it is easier to get six new white rhinos than six new, really good-quality, blood-curdling ghosts. Ours does its best but it isn't good enough. It lays its wet hands on my face and on other people's faces but this is rather a feeble performance. It is too good-natured. Ours is a dull ghost.

Some years ago we called in a ghost expert. I think she was a professional witch of some sort. Witches are less numerous and less talked about than they were a few hundred years ago but they still exist. Indeed they are quite powerful and have their own trade union. Our ghost expert (I should be careful about calling her a witch because I cannot quite remember all the fine distinctions, and while witches are proud of being called witches, ordinary women as a rule are not too keen on being so described) – so our ghost expert came to discover whether we had any more ghosts around the house. I told her that we were not aware of any others roaming about along with our old resident. She gave me a slightly contemptuous 'What do you know?' type of look and began work. Soon she reported that we had nine other ghosts in the house. This was something of a surprise, but an expert is an expert.

Now ghosts, as every decent person knows, are creatures in need of help. They want to pass on and they are entitled to their proper rest. The lady said she would do what she could and she was most successful. She helped the nine newly discovered ghosts most efficiently. Their passing on made little difference to us, since we hadn't known they were there, but no doubt it was of great benefit to them. The ghost expert then collected her fee and passed on too, to her next assignment. The only person who stayed was our original ghost, and he is still with us.

We do not know much about him; his history is shrouded in mystery. Long ago a cruel murder was committed in our park and he is supposed to have been the

I have ghost-appeal and they cling to me

victim. As I have said, he (or she – one does not know much about the sex of a ghost; indeed, the sex-life of ghosts is the only kind still unexplored) touches my face, opens doors, closes doors, brushes against me and performs similar feeble tricks. It is all my fault. I am a natural medium. I have ghost-appeal and they swarm about me. I may not be particularly popular with people, but ghosts just love me.

Eighteen years ago I was living in South Africa. Suddenly and unexpectedly I heard the news that my father was dead. I had to leave for England then and there, without being able to shut up the house properly, or even put things away. I always wanted to go back to that South African house but I could not manage it until last year. Then I did return and it was a most peculiar and eerie experience. Everything was just as I had left it eighteen years before: cups and forks and knives as they had been hurriedly put down; my ex-wife's jars of make-up and bottles of perfume on the dressing-table; shoes lying in odd places; clothes hanging in the cupboards; old letters in the drawers; a few others on the desk, piled up there waiting to be answered but the answers had never been written and the ink had dried in the ink-pot.

My reason for returning after eighteen years was simply to pack. I was doing this job when I realized I was becoming slightly irritated by the noise of the cars which kept arriving and driving away again, and the children playing. There is nothing sensational or even remarkable in cars arriving at a place, but I thought (it was no more

On ghosts

than a passing and almost unregistered thought at the time) that there were rather a lot of cars coming and going considering what a small derelict place it was. And also there seemed to be rather a lot of children, making a little bit more noise than was agreeable. But neither the cars nor the children really troubled me and I went on packing and clearing away my things.

Having almost finished my task, I went outside but saw no cars and no children. Not one car, not one child. This seemed odd after all those comings and goings and after all that happy laughter. But the cars could have gone and so could the children. Then I saw the dour, elderly Afrikaner who looked after the house while occupying another part of it, and who was standing there, waiting for me. I looked at him questioningly but his face remained impassive, so I had to ask him: had he, too, heard the cars coming and going? Oh, yes, he had. And the children playing and making a lot of noise? Yes, he'd heard the children too. Well then, where were the cars and the children? He shook his head. There were no cars and no children. Only the noise.

I was taken aback and wanted a little more explanation but none was forthcoming. He simply shrugged his shoulders. It was always like that. One always heard the noise of cars and the laughter of children but there were no cars and no children. One got used to it and that was all. There was nothing more to discuss.

I returned to give the finishing touches to my packing and at once heard the voices again. As soon as I heard them, I rushed out to see if I could catch a glimpse of either a car or a child. I could see neither. Four times I ran out and four times was confronted with total emptiness and solitude.

How do I explain it? I do not and cannot. I can only say that it happened. The old Afrikaner, by taking it in such a matter-of-fact manner, made the whole experience even weirder but brought me no nearer to a solution.

Another time when my ghost-appeal worked rather disconcertingly was one evening, some years ago, while I was staying with friends and a few of us were sitting round a big log-fire. Our host was an odd man who used to read people's palms with passionate interest and tell their fortunes. We were discussing ghosts and their ways when suddenly the room began to grow cooler and cooler. This was quite noticeable and happened in an incredibly short time. Within a few minutes all of us, about five people, were shivering, our teeth chattering. The cold in the room became biting. And yet, the huge log fire was burning as merrily as before.

These were eerie experiences. A ghost or two is welcome. It does have a chilling effect, but this kind of central chilling is as indispensable in a Stately Home as central heating is in a private house. You can, however, have too much of a good thing and I would not be keen on living with the noises of non-existent cars and non-existent children; neither would I care to freeze too often in front of a large and merrily crackling log fire.

Some of my readers may shake their heads and say:

On ghosts

'Funny. I'd never have expected *him* to believe in that sort of thing.'

I'd never have expected it myself. The truth is, indeed, that I do not believe in that sort of thing. I am sure there is a perfectly reasonable, rational and scientific explanation for it all. But I do not know what it is.

In the meantime try to acquire a harmless, quiet, good-natured ghost like mine. And never mind if he is a bit of a bore.

On lions and monkeys

Henry Bath, who runs Longleat so successfully, has borrowed one or two ideas of mine. In retaliation I have pinched his best idea and I am most grateful to him.

I opened a Game Reserve, as he had done, and I do advise all beginners to do the same. Here again, a larger place is better than a smaller. You cannot keep too many lions in a three-room flat. Even in a small house a hundred monkeys might prove too many.

Not so long ago I found myself in a difficult situation. I had vast debts and was in grave financial difficulties. I felt lost. I had toyed with the idea of a Game Park for some time and I felt that now I had to take the plunge. It was no easy decision and I was scared.

I got hold of the animals, hiring my lions and other livestock, and spent £20,000 in three months on television advertising. I am used to free publicity and did not part with the money lightheartedly. But I had no choice.

My preparations had been thorough and I had supplied plenty of animals. I can claim that my visitors can see more lions and other wild animals in natural-seeming surroundings in my Game Park in one hour than they can in the most famous South African game reserve in two days.* But however well prepared I was, the nagging doubt remained; would the crowds come? They did. They turned up the very first weekend and things have never looked back since. The Game Park solved all my problems. I was able to settle my debts and for the first time my bank balance is comfortably in the black. It is a strange feeling but no doubt one gets used to it in time.

The entrance fee to the Game Park is £1 per car, no matter how many people it contains. I was watching the arrivals that first weekend and was pleased. People were pouring in. Then I saw four cars draw up, full of Pakistanis. The passengers got out of three of the cars and piled into the fourth on top of all the people who were already in there. The car looked like the black hole of Calcutta. But they were welcome and still are to this day. If they want to save money, they are fully entitled to do so: the entrance fee remains £1 per car.

The Game Park brought some new problems and opened up some new situations for me. There have to be watchtowers and hunters armed with shotguns all over the place, to protect the sightseers. People are safe enough there, although they frequently do their level best to endanger themselves.

On one occasion a child was playing with the electric cigarette lighter in a car and set his clothes alight.

'We were in a difficult situation,' his father told me

---

* A new and surprising item of export is British-bred lions to African game reserves; they have a better sense of show-biz than the native product.

On lions and monkeys

subsequently. 'We didn't know what to do. I thought of throwing the child out but my wife disapproved.'

The rule is that in an emergency – should your car break down, for instance, or run out of petrol – you stop the car, sound the horn and wait for help. It will arrive in no time. These rules are conspicuously displayed, everyone knows them but few obey them. When visitors are in trouble, they always get out of their cars. They get out in order to fix a wind-screen wiper or just to admire the scenery. Some want to show off and prove that they are made of sterner stuff and are not afraid of a mere lion. Most of them are just thoughtless. What do you do when your wind-screen wiper stops functioning? You get out and adjust it. Besides, these lions and other wild animals look so harmless and innocent.

Motor-bikes are not allowed in, which surprises some people. They regard it as unfair discrimination against motor bikes, a conspiracy of the rich against the poor, a prejudice of the haughty aristocracy against the working class.

'Some motor bikes are faster than cars,' they keep explaining.

'But some cheetahs are faster than motor bikes,' my men reply.

Open sports cars are not allowed in either, nor are cars with canvas tops. The lions are playful and are accustomed to jumping on the bonnets and roofs of cars. They do no damage and children (grown-ups too, for that matter) are delighted when they do so. But a couple with a child

'But some cheetahs are faster than motorbikes'

On lions and monkeys

visiting another Game Park were less delighted when a lion jumped on the roof of their canvas-topped car, and fell through it. The husband and wife were occupying the front seats and the lion found itself sitting on the back seat, next to the child.

'It was a painful experience,' the owner of that Stately Game Park commented. 'The poor lion got a terrible shock.'

The shock suffered by the lion was fortunately the worst effect of that particular incident. The people were lucky.

One hot day a woman accompanied by her seven-year-old child came to my Game Park. Although the regulations make it quite clear that the windows must be kept shut, she opened one. She was warned at once that it was dangerous. She shut her window and drove on. As soon as the hunters were out of sight, she opened her window again. This sequence was repeated three times. Suddenly there was a terrifying shriek. The child had been sitting on the edge of the open window when a lion had crept or leaped up and had bitten a piece out of the child's bottom. A horrible thing which should never have happened. When the woman was subsequently asked why had she opened the window in spite of repeated warnings, she explained: 'It was very hot.'

(One reason why you must keep the windows closed is that the smell of human flesh and blood excites wild animals. With the windows shut they do not scent it.)

You get various surprises when you are a new Game

How to run a Stately Home

Park owner and know a little less about wild life than you ought to. I ordered a number of white rhinos and when they arrived I was bitterly disappointed by their lack of whiteness. I thought of trying out various washing powders on them, but was informed by the experts that nothing would help. Luckily, no one has asked for his money back as yet on the grounds that my rhinos are not white enough.

When these white rhinos arrived, my wife decided to have a ride on one. I thought it a somewhat reckless decision but she told me that she had never ridden a rhinoceros – white or black – before, and, of course, a man must have a heart. She rode the rhino magnificently and after that it was named Nicole, after her. The Duchess found it, at first, a doubtful compliment but ultimately she became convinced that it *was* a compliment. She is still very fond of her namesake but has never used it as a mount again.

The rhinos and elephants are peaceful and harmless but we had to build double iron gates inside the reserve itself for those wilder and more dangerous animals, the big cats. I have already mentioned that my weekly butcher's bill for the lions runs up to £1,000. The cheetahs eat chicken meat and they, too, have healthy appetites. But with about 1,200,000 visitors a year (and their number still growing) they may indulge in their daily meat.

Monkeys provide the greatest attraction of all, so lay in a lot of them. I have about two hundred and fifty of them and they roam all over the place. They are cheaper to buy

On lions and monkeys

and cheaper to feed than lions, and they steal the show every time. They gambol all around you, jump on the car, pull faces, make love, swing from branches and do all the things you expect monkeys to do. Even the most expensive monkey is dirt cheap compared to a big cat. They are all worth their weight in gold and sure to be a great success.

I often have the feeling that they are watching us as we are watching them, and are just as amused by our antics as we are by theirs. They find us just as odd and comic as we find them. And they have a final laugh up their sleeve because they do not have to pay one single penny for the entertainment we afford them.

Fishing

I like to act the cynic and used to be amused by the low opinions expressed about my sordid commercial approach to running my business. I quite enjoyed my reputation, but nowadays I hear less and less about it. This saddens me a little, but it is true. I have the frightful feeling that I am becoming respectable. A place visited by about 1,200,000 people a year is Big Business, and present-day nobility, high society, aristocracy – call them what you like – respect nothing so much as they respect cash and a big turnover. As I respect them myself, there is nothing I can do against my growing respectability. I must accept it with a sigh. The best thing I can do is to preach my doctrine, disseminate my wisdom and give advice to newcomers. This I have done in the present volume.

My own favourites of all my visitors, are the anglers. People who want to fish pay £1 to come and fish all day in my lake. They may catch as many fish as they like. The only snag is that before they depart they have to throw every one of them back into the water. Which they do dutifully.

I am somewhat amazed by them. Why do they come? What's the point? But they don't only come, they queue

Throw every one of them back into the water

Fishing

up. In my more profound moods I think: such is life, isn't that what we are all doing? All of us, without exception? We pay our entrance fee, spend a busy day fishing, then when we have caught as much as we can in that short time, we throw the fish back and depart. It may be a little pointless, but if we can enjoy it as much as the anglers evidently do it cannot be called a waste of time.

Postscript

In conclusion, and seriously: if you have a large family house which is hard to keep up, love it and want to preserve it, do open it. Do it in the right spirit, as you would if you were inviting friends to stay. The people who will come to see it, will be full of expectancy, so be warm, try to make your house seem welcoming and friendly, and you will be astonished at the appreciation given in return.

I know that I have learnt the most important lesson of my life from opening Woburn. It is that the pleasure you give to other people is the most rewarding thing in the world. And there are few things which give more pleasure of many different kinds, to more people, than a well organized and generously shared Stately Home.